Empathy

Ashley Lee

Explore other books at:
WWW.ENGAGEBOOKS.COM

VANCOUVER, B.C.

 WWW.ENGAGEBOOKS.COM

Empathy: Good Character Traits
Lee, Ashley, 1995 –
Text © 2024 Engage Books
Design © 2024 Engage Books

Edited by: A.R. Roumanis
Design by: Mandy Christiansen

Text set in Myriad Pro Regular.
Chapter headings set in Anton.

FIRST EDITION / FIRST PRINTING

All rights reserved. No part of this book may be stored in a retrieval system, reproduced or transmitted in any form or by any other means without written permission from the publisher or a licence from the Canadian Copyright Licensing Agency. Critics and reviewers may quote brief passages in connection with a review or critical article in any media.

Every reasonable effort has been made to contact the copyright holders of all material reproduced in this book.

LIBRARY AND ARCHIVES CANADA CATALOGUING IN PUBLICATION

Title: Empathy / Ashley Lee.
Names: Lee, Ashley, author.
Description: Series statement: Good Character Traits

ISBN 978-1-77878-655-6 (hardcover)
ISBN 978-1-77878-656-3 (softcover)
ISBN 978-1-77878-657-0 (epub)
ISBN 978-1-77878-658-7 (pdf)

This project has been made possible in part by the Government of Canada.

Empathy

Contents

- 4 What Is Empathy?
- 6 Why Is Empathy Important?
- 8 What Does Empathy Look Like?
- 10 How Does Empathy Affect You?
- 12 How Does Empathy Affect Others?
- 14 Does Everyone Feel Empathy?
- 16 Is It Bad if You Do Not Feel Empathy?
- 18 Does Empathy Change Over Time?
- 20 Is It Hard to Feel Empathy?
- 22 How Can You Learn to Have More Empathy?
- 24 How Can You Help Others Have More Empathy?
- 26 How to Feel Empathy Every Day
- 28 Empathy Around the World
- 30 Quiz

What Is Empathy?

Empathy is when you understand how someone else feels.

Empathy

It means sharing other people's happiness or sadness.

5

Why Is Empathy Important?

Empathy helps you connect with other people.

Empathy

This helps people become better friends.

What Does Empathy Look Like?

People who feel empathy listen when other people talk.

Empathy

They offer to help when someone is sad or needs **support**.

Key Word

Support: be there for someone when they need help.

How Does Empathy Affect You?

Empathy helps you be a better friend.

Empathy

It helps you understand how other people see the world.

How Does Empathy Affect Others?

Feeling empathy makes other people feel loved.

Empathy

They know that you really **care** about them.

Key Word

Care: like someone and want them to be happy.

Does Everyone Feel Empathy?

Most people do feel empathy.

Empathy

But sometimes people forget to feel empathy.

15

Is It Bad if You Do Not Feel Empathy?

It is okay if you do not always feel empathy.

Empathy

Sometimes it takes **practice** to feel empathy.

Key Word

Practice: do something over and over again so you get better at it.

Does Empathy Change Over Time?

Many people feel more empathy as they get older.

Empathy

Some people start to feel less empathy if other people have let them down.

Is It Hard to Feel Empathy?

It can be hard to feel empathy if you do not like someone.

Empathy

You do not have to feel empathy. But you should still be kind.

How Can You Learn to Have More Empathy?

Pay attention to how other people are feeling.

Empathy

Think about how you might feel if you were them.

How Can You Help Others Have More Empathy?

Share how you feel with other people.

Empathy

Be an **example** by showing other people empathy.

Key Word

Example: a way to show something to help someone understand.

How to Feel Empathy Every Day

1. Ask other people how they are feeling.

2. Listen to what other people are saying.

Empathy

3. Celebrate other people when they do well.

4. Offer to help when you see someone having a hard time.

Key Word

Celebrate: do something fun for a special event.

Empathy Around the World

Some people do not have enough food to eat.

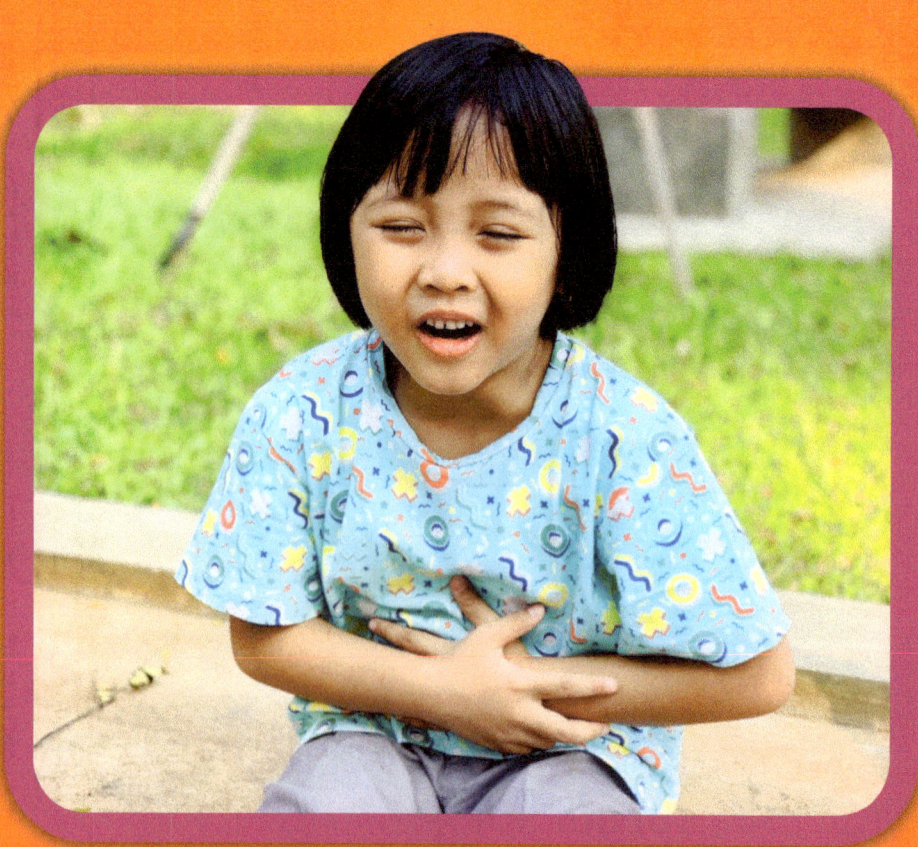

Empathy

People all over the world give food to **food banks** so people have enough to eat.

Key Word

Food banks: places where people in need can go to get free food.

Quiz

Test your knowledge of empathy by answering the following questions. The questions are based on what you have read in this book. The answers are listed on the bottom of the next page.

1 Does empathy help you connect with other people?

2 Do people who feel empathy listen when other people talk?

3 Does empathy help you be a better friend?

4 Do most people feel empathy?

5 Is it okay if you do not always feel empathy?

6 Should you pay attention to how other people are feeling?

30

Explore Other Pre-1 Readers.

Visit www.engagebooks.com/readers

Answers: 1. Yes 2. Yes 3. Yes 4. Yes 5. Yes 6. Yes

Milton Keynes UK
Ingram Content Group UK Ltd.
UKHW051106141024
449707UK00017B/196